Holt Spanish 1

Independent Study Guide

HOLT, RINEHART AND WINSTON

A Harcourt Education Company

Orlando • **Austin** • New York • San Diego • Toronto • London

Table of Contents

To the Student

Whether you are studying *¡Exprésate!* on your own, learning Spanish in an independent-study course at school, or have been absent and need to catch up, this *Independent Study Guide* will prove a valuable tool for you. It will help you learn the material in every chapter of *¡Exprésate!* It is also an excellent way to prepare for tests and exams.

The **Study Tips** in the first section are listed by chapter. They contain ideas for increasing your learning power and suggestions for practicing in different ways.

The key to successful independent study is organization. Just as a teacher plans and organizes his or her classes or an engineer programs the steps in building a bridge on a particular site, you need to make a study plan and stick to it. In this book, you will find monthly **Student Planners** to help you organize your independent study. Program the steps to complete your tasks day-by-day on the lines provided for every school day of the month.

The **Checklists** for each chapter are divided into sections that match the textbook. The items in the checklist will indicate what you should study and read in each chapter of *¡Exprésate!* in order to cover the material and which activities in the textbook you should do to practice and learn the material. Some activities found in the textbook are not included here because they require work with a partner or in groups. For the listening activities, use the online textbook.

After each two-page checklist, there is a chapter **Self-Test,** which consists of a series of questions that focus on the *¡Exprésate!* expressions. First answer aloud; then write your answer. If you cannot give the correct answer and have to look back in the textbook, or if you take a long time to come up with the answer, that tells you that you need to review that material.

To wrap up a chapter, turn to the **Fold-n-Learn Project** for an enjoyable change of pace. With the help of easy-to-follow instructions and drawings, you can turn a sheet of paper into a study aid. This might be a small book or a pyramid or a pleated shade. As you create the suggested project, you will review important parts of the chapter. Once you have completed the project, you will have a study aid that you can use again and again.

(iv)

Study Tips

Chapter 1

Before giving a talk, often people will stand in front of a mirror to practice. It's natural and normal, so don't be shy about practicing your Spanish that way. Look in the mirror and introduce yourself in Spanish. Don't forget to smile! Still looking in the mirror, practice greeting someone and asking how he or she is. Try to do it two different ways. One way is using the informal **tú** form and the other way is the formal **usted** form you use with a teacher or other adult. You'll use the two ways of saying "you" in Spanish in every chapter.

Chapter 2

Flip through magazines and use Spanish to describe the people in the pictures. Don't just think the description; say it. Magazines for teenagers often have pictures of the musicians, celebrities, and electronic products that you either like or don't like. Express this aloud in Spanish. The advertising sections of the Sunday paper have pictures of food and products that you can also describe and tell whether you like them or not. You will be using masculine and feminine forms as well as singular and plural.

Chapter 3

If you follow all the steps in the checklists, you'll be making flashcards for sports and activities in this chapter. Making flashcards is an excellent way to learn new words. On one side, you'll write the Spanish word or phrase you want to learn. The other side can have a drawing (the suggestion for this chapter) or the English equivalent. You don't have to be an artist to draw on a flashcard. Just do a simple sketch. After all, you're the only one who'll see it.

Chapter 4

Here's a suggestion for learning the Spanish words for nouns. Always say and write the article—**el** or **la**—along with the noun. That way you'll learn the difference that Spanish makes between masculine and feminine nouns as you learn the meaning. You need to know a noun's gender so that you can make a descriptive word agree with the noun. This is called gender agreement. A masculine adjective goes with a masculine noun, while feminine adjectives go with feminine nouns. Agreement in number, on the other hand, means using singular or plural forms of the article—**los** or **las**—and of descriptive words.

Chapter 5

To learn the meaning of new verbs, you can make flashcards. But to really learn a verb, it isn't enough just to know the infinitive. Say and write out the complete conjugation. Some students remember better if they associate verb forms with gestures or movements. For example, point to yourself with your thumb or finger when you say the **yo** form. Then point directly in front of you with a smile on your face when you say the **tú** form. Point again with a more serious look for the **usted** form; then point off in another direction to use the same form with **él** and **ella.** Work out your own system of gestures for all the forms.

Chapter 6

Learning Spanish challenges you to express yourself in ways that are different from English. Spanish isn't just different words; it's a new way of looking at things. You've already dealt with two ways of saying "you" and with nouns having gender and with the need to have agreement in gender and number. Now you're tackling the rather amazing idea that there are two ways to express "to be." Pay special attention to the parts in the checklists on **ser** and **estar** and practice saying all the examples and activities with these verbs in the textbook. That way, you'll be off to a good start.

Chapter 7

One way to learn to talk about your daily routine in Spanish is to say the steps of your routine aloud in Spanish while you're doing them. You might feel a little silly talking to yourself, but you will remember the expressions much better this way than by simply memorizing.

Chapter 8

You can use catalogs or the advertisements in the newspaper to practice talking about clothes. Do you know someone else who is studying Spanish? Why not call him or her on the phone and talk in Spanish about what each of you is wearing? You might throw in a little harmless gossip about a mutual friend who was wearing something that didn't fit. Maybe the two of you could arrange to get together and go shopping in Spanish. Don't be afraid to make mistakes. This kind of informal, one-on-one practice can be both fun and productive.

Chapter 9

Try to schedule your time so that you study some in the textbook every day. You will learn more and learn it better this way than by spending a longer time on just one or two days a week. In addition to the textbook, you can look for different ways to have contact with Spanish. The more contact you have, the easier learning becomes. Magazines and television programs in Spanish are available almost everywhere. You won't understand all the words at this stage, but you'll pick up more of the flavor and tone of Spanish, especially on TV, where the human interaction, facial expressions, and body language will help you understand more.

Chapter 10

In each chapter in *¡Exprésate!* you've learned about a different part of the Spanish-speaking world, including parts of this country with large Spanish-speaking populations. You can go online to find out more about the places that interested you most. Many Web sites let you select the language you want to proceed in, just like ATM machines do. Choose Spanish, and do some armchair traveling in your new language. When you are in an airport, notice the bilingual signs and information. At every turn, it seems increasingly clear that the future belongs to the person who knows both English and Spanish.

Use these monthly planners to help plan your day-by-day activities.

agosto

1 _____

2 _____

3 _____

4 _____

5 _____

6 _____

7 _____

8 _____

9 _____

10 _____

11 _____

12 _____

13 _____

14 _____

15 _____

16 _____

17 _____

18 _____

19 _____

20 _____

21 _____

22 _____

23 _____

24 _____

25 _____

26 _____

27 _____

28 _____

29 _____

30 _____

31 _____

Holt Spanish 1   Independent Study Guide

septiembre

1 _____

2 _____

3 _____

4 _____

5 _____

6 _____

7 _____

8 _____

9 _____

10 _____

11 _____

12 _____

13 _____

14 _____

15 _____

16 _____

17 _____

18 _____

19 _____

20 _____

21 _____

22 _____

23 _____

24 _____

25 _____

26 _____

27 _____

28 _____

29 _____

30 _____

octubre

1 _____
2 _____
3 _____
4 _____
5 _____
6 _____
7 _____
8 _____
9 _____
10 _____
11 _____
12 _____
13 _____
14 _____
15 _____
16 _____
17 _____
18 _____
19 _____
20 _____
21 _____
22 _____
23 _____
24 _____
25 _____
26 _____
27 _____
28 _____
29 _____
30 _____
31 _____

noviembre

1 _____
2 _____
3 _____
4 _____
5 _____
6 _____
7 _____
8 _____
9 _____
10 _____
11 _____
12 _____
13 _____
14 _____
15 _____
16 _____
17 _____
18 _____
19 _____
20 _____
21 _____
22 _____
23 _____
24 _____
25 _____
26 _____
27 _____
28 _____
29 _____
30 _____

Holt Spanish 1

Independent Study Guide

1 _____

2 _____

3 _____

4 _____

5 _____

6 _____

7 _____

8 _____

9 _____

10 _____

11 _____

12 _____

13 _____

14 _____

15 _____

16 _____

17 _____

18 _____

19 _____

20 _____

21 _____

22 _____

23 _____

24 _____

25 _____

26 _____

27 _____

28 _____

29 _____

30 _____

31 _____

xi

enero

1 _____
2 _____
3 _____
4 _____
5 _____
6 _____
7 _____
8 _____
9 _____
10 _____
11 _____
12 _____
13 _____
14 _____
15 _____
16 _____
17 _____
18 _____
19 _____
20 _____
21 _____
22 _____
23 _____
24 _____
25 _____
26 _____
27 _____
28 _____
29 _____
30 _____
31 _____

febrero

1 _____

2 _____

3 _____

4 _____

5 _____

6 _____

7 _____

8 _____

9 _____

10 _____

11 _____

12 _____

13 _____

14 _____

15 _____

16 _____

17 _____

18 _____

19 _____

20 _____

21 _____

22 _____

23 _____

24 _____

25 _____

26 _____

27 _____

28 _____

[29 _____]

marzo

1 _____
2 _____
3 _____
4 _____
5 _____
6 _____
7 _____
8 _____
9 _____
10 _____
11 _____
12 _____
13 _____
14 _____
15 _____
16 _____
17 _____
18 _____
19 _____
20 _____
21 _____
22 _____
23 _____
24 _____
25 _____
26 _____
27 _____
28 _____
29 _____
30 _____
31 _____

Holt Spanish 1

abril

1 _____
2 _____
3 _____
4 _____
5 _____
6 _____
7 _____
8 _____
9 _____
10 _____
11 _____
12 _____
13 _____
14 _____
15 _____
16 _____
17 _____
18 _____
19 _____
20 _____
21 _____
22 _____
23 _____
24 _____
25 _____
26 _____
27 _____
28 _____
29 _____
30 _____

mayo

1 _____
2 _____
3 _____
4 _____
5 _____
6 _____
7 _____
8 _____
9 _____
10 _____
11 _____
12 _____
13 _____
14 _____
15 _____
16 _____
17 _____
18 _____
19 _____
20 _____
21 _____
22 _____
23 _____
24 _____
25 _____
26 _____
27 _____
28 _____
29 _____
30 _____
31 _____

Holt Spanish 1

junio

1 _____
2 _____
3 _____
4 _____
5 _____
6 _____
7 _____
8 _____
9 _____
10 _____
11 _____
12 _____
13 _____
14 _____
15 _____
16 _____
17 _____
18 _____
19 _____
20 _____
21 _____
22 _____
23 _____
24 _____
25 _____
26 _____
27 _____
28 _____
29 _____
30 _____

julio

1 _____
2 _____
3 _____
4 _____
5 _____
6 _____
7 _____
8 _____
9 _____
10 _____
11 _____
12 _____
13 _____
14 _____
15 _____
16 _____
17 _____
18 _____
19 _____
20 _____
21 _____
22 _____
23 _____
24 _____
25 _____
26 _____
27 _____
28 _____
29 _____
30 _____
31 _____

¡TU LIBRO ES UN COFRE DE TESORO!

(Your book is a treasure chest!)

Each chapter in *¡Exprésate!* has the same parts or sections. Getting to know this structure will help you to plan your independent study and also to study for quizzes and exams. With the help of a parent or guardian, search your *¡Exprésate!* textbook for the titles on the pages in the questions below. After filling in the puzzle with the titles, you will be able to discover the hidden message. The message will give you the key to open the *¡Exprésate!* Treasure Chest.

Find the answers to these questions; then write your answers in the puzzle on the next page. For example, the answer to question 2 is **Vocabulario en acción.** NOTE: The answers are not in the same order as the questions.

1. What is the name of the section that introduces you to Spain?
2. What chapter section starts on page 6?
3. What is the name of the box on page 7?
4. What chapter section starts on page 12?
5. What is the name of the box on page 14?
6. What is the name of the box at the top of page 21?
7. What is the name of the review box on page 24?
8. What is the title of the second activity on page 25?
9. What starts on page 30?
10. What is the name of the box on page 31?
11. What section starts on page 32?
12. What starts on page 36?

Fill in the blanks with the answers to the questions.

6. ¡ ☐☐◯☐☐☐☐☐ !

4. ☐◯☐☐☐☐☐☐■☐☐■☐☐☐☐☐☐

9. ☐☐☐☐☐☐■☐■☐☐☐☐☐☐◯☐☐

1. ☐☐☐◯☐☐☐☐☐☐

10. ☐☐☐☐☐☐■☐☐☐■☐☐☐☐☐◯☐☐

12. ☐☐☐☐☐☐☐☐☐◯☐☐

2. | V | o | c | a | b | u | l | a | r | i | o | ■ | e | n | ■ | a | c | c | i | ó | n |

7. ¿ ☐☐■☐☐☐◯☐☐☐ ?

8. ☐☐☐☐☐☐◯☐☐☐☐☐

5. ☐☐■☐☐☐☐◯☐☐

11. ☐☐☐☐☐◯

3. ☐☐☐☐■☐☐☐◯☐☐☐☐

Now copy the circled letters in these blanks in the same order they appear in the puzzle. What is the hidden message?

☐☐☐☐☐☐☐☐■☐■☐☐☐ !

Holt Spanish 1

Chapter Resources

¡Empecemos!

CAPÍTULO

CHAPTER CHECKLIST

Geocultura
☐ Read and study the information on Spain in **Geocultura,** pp. xxiv–3.

Vocabulario 1
☐ Study the expressions in **¡Exprésate!,** p. 6, to learn how to ask someone's name and give your name and others' names.

☐ Read about nicknames and expressing affection with -**ito** and -**ita** in **Nota cultural,** p. 7.

☐ Use the online textbook to do listening Activity 1, p. 7.

☐ Do Activities 2–3, p. 7, in writing.

☐ Study the greetings and goodbyes in **Más vocabulario,** p. 8.

☐ Study the expressions in **¡Exprésate!,** p. 8, to learn how to ask how someone is and to say how you are.

☐ Use the online textbook to do listening Activity 5, p. 9.

☐ Write out Activities 6–8, p. 9.

☐ Study the expressions in **¡Exprésate!** and **Más vocabulario,** p. 10, to learn how to introduce others and respond to introductions.

☐ Do Activity 9, p. 10.

☐ Study the expressions in **¡Exprésate!,** p. 11, to learn how to ask where someone is from and tell where you and others are from.

☐ Use the online textbook to do listening Activity 10, p. 11.

☐ Do Activity 11, p. 11, in writing.

☐ For additional practice with **Vocabulario 1,** do the activities on pp. 1–3 in the *Cuaderno de vocabulario y gramática.*

Gramática 1
☐ Study the presentation on subjects and verbs in sentences, p. 12.

☐ Read about titles when addressing people in **Nota cultural,** p. 12.

☐ Do Activities 13–14, pp. 12–13, in writing.

☐ Study the presentation on subject pronouns and read **En inglés,** p. 14.

☐ Do Activity 16, p. 14, in writing.

☐ Use the online textbook to do listening Activity 17, p. 15.

☐ Do Activity 18, p. 15.

☐ For additional practice with **Gramática 1,** do the activities on pp. 4–6 in the *Cuaderno de vocabulario y gramática* and on pp. 1–3 in the *Cuaderno de actividades.*

1

CHAPTER CHECKLIST

Vocabulario 2

☐ Study the words in **Vocabulario 2** and **Más vocabulario,** p. 18, to learn numbers.

☐ Do Activities 20–21, p. 18.

☐ Study the expressions in **¡Exprésate!,** p. 19, to learn how to ask for and give phone numbers.

☐ Use the online textbook to do listening Activity 22, p. 19.

☐ Study **¿Qué hora es?,** p. 20, to learn how to ask for and give the time.

☐ Do Activities 25–26, p. 20.

☐ Study the expressions in **¡Exprésate!,** p. 21, to learn how to ask for and give the date and day of the week.

☐ Do Activity 27, p. 21.

☐ Study **el alfabeto,** p. 22.

☐ Study the expressions in **¡Exprésate!,** p. 23, to learn how to ask how words are spelled and to give e-mail addresses.

☐ Use the online textbook to do listening Activity 29, p. 23.

☐ For additional practice with **Vocabulario 2,** do the activities on pp. 7–9 in the *Cuaderno de vocabulario y gramática.*

Gramática 2

☐ Study the presentation on the present tense of the verb **ser** and read **¿Te acuerdas?,** p. 24.

☐ Do Activities 32–34, pp. 24–25.

☐ Study the presentation on punctuation marks and written accents, p. 26.

☐ Write Activities 36–38, pp. 26–27.

☐ For additional practice with **Gramática 2,** do the activities on pp. 10–12 in the *Cuaderno de vocabulario y gramática* and on pp. 5–7 in the *Cuaderno de actividades.*

2

¡Empecemos!

1. Can you ask someone's name and give your name? (p. 6)

   • How would you ask a classmate his or her name?
   • How would you give your name?
   • How would you ask an adult's name?
   • How would you ask who someone is?
   • How would you say who someone is?

2. Can you greet someone and say goodbye? (p. 8)

   • How would you greet and say good-bye to your teacher?

3. Can you ask how someone is and tell how you are? (p. 8)

   • How would you ask your teacher how he or she is?
   • How would you tell how you are?

4. Can you introduce someone and respond to an introduction? (p. 10)

   • How would you introduce a class-mate to your teacher?
   • How would you respond to an intro-duction?

5. Can you ask where someone is from and tell where you are from? (p. 11)

   • How would you ask a classmate where he or she is from?
   • How would you tell where you are from?

6. Can you ask for someone's phone number and give yours? (p. 19)

   • How would you ask a classmate his or her phone number?
   • How would you tell your phone number?

7. Can you ask and tell what time it is? (p. 20)

   • How would you ask what time it is?
   • How would you say the time now?

8. Can you ask and answer about the date and day of the week? (p. 21)

   • How would you say today's date?
   • How would you ask what day it is?

9. Can you ask for someone's e-mail address and give yours? (p. 23)

   • How would you ask a classmate his or her e-mail address?
   • How would you say your e-mail address?

3

A conocernos

Geocultura

☐ Read and study the information on Puerto Rico in **Geocultura**, pp. 38–41.

Vocabulario 1

☐ Study the words in **Vocabulario 1** and **Más vocabulario**, pp. 44–45, to learn adjectives to describe someone.

☐ Study the expressions in **¡Exprésate!**, p. 45, to learn how to ask what someone is like and to describe someone.

☐ Read about describing skin and hair color in **Nota Cultural**, p. 46.

☐ Do Activities 1 and 3, p. 46, in writing.

☐ Use the online textbook to do listening Activity 3, p. 46.

☐ Study the words and expressions in **¡Exprésate!**, p. 47, to learn how to ask and tell someone's age and birthday.

☐ Study the words in **Más vocabulario**, p. 47, to learn more numbers.

☐ Do Activity 4, p. 47.

☐ For additional practice with **Vocabulario 1,** do the activities on pp. 13–15 in the *Cuaderno de vocabulario y gramática.*

Gramática 1

☐ Study the presentation on **ser** with adjectives and read **¿Te acuerdas?**, p. 48.

☐ Do Activities 7–9, pp. 48–49, in writing.

☐ Study the presentation on gender and adjective agreement, p. 50.

☐ Do Activities 11–13, pp. 50–51, in writing.

☐ Study the presentation on question formation and read **¿Te acuerdas?**, p. 52.

☐ Use the online textbook to do listening Activity 15, p. 52.

☐ Do Activities 16–18, pp. 52–53.

☐ Read about turning 18 in Puerto Rico in **Nota Cultural,** p. 53.

☐ For additional practice with **Gramática 1,** do the activities on pp. 16–18 in the *Cuaderno de vocabulario y gramática* and on pp. 11–13 in the *Cuaderno de actividades.*

   4

CHAPTER CHECKLIST

Vocabulario 2

☐ Study the words and expressions in **Vocabulario 2,** pp. 56–57, to learn to say what you like.

☐ Study the expressions in **¡Exprésate!,** p. 57, to learn how to ask someone what he or she likes and to respond.

☐ Read about music and musicians in Puerto Rico in **Nota cultural,** p. 58.

☐ Do Activity 20, p. 58.

☐ Use the online textbook to do listening Activity 21, p. 58.

☐ Study the expressions in **¡Exprésate!,** p. 58, to learn how to describe something.

☐ Do Activity 22, p. 59.

☐ Do Activity 23, p. 59, in writing.

☐ For additional practice with **Vocabulario 2,** do the activities on pp. 19–21 in the *Cuaderno de vocabulario y gramática.*

Gramática 2

☐ Study the presentation on nouns and definite articles and read **En inglés,** p. 60.

☐ Write Activities 25–26, p. 61.

☐ Study the presentation on the verb **gustar, ¿por qué?,** and **porque,** and read **En inglés,** p. 62.

☐ Use the online textbook to do listening Activity 28, p. 62.

☐ Do Activity 29, p. 63, in writing.

☐ Study the presentation on the preposition **de,** and read **En inglés,** p. 64.

☐ Do Activity 32, p. 64.

☐ Write Activity 33, p. 65.

☐ Use the online textbook to do listening Activity 34, p. 65.

☐ For additional practice, do the activities on pp. 22–24 in the *Cuaderno de vocabulario y gramática* and on pp. 15–17 in the *Cuaderno de actividades.*

5

A conocernos

1. Can you ask what someone is like and describe someone? (p. 45)	• How would you ask a classmate what his or her best friend is like? • How would you describe what your best friend is like?
2. Can you ask and tell someone's age and birthday? (p. 47)	• How would you ask a classmate how old he or she is? • How would you ask when his or her birthday is? • How would you ask him or her how old another classmate is? • How would you tell your age and birthday? • How would you tell a friend's age and birthday?
3. Can you ask someone what he or she likes and tell what you like and don't like? (p. 57)	• How would you ask a classmate if he or she likes something? • How would you ask a friend what he or she likes more? • How would you say you like something?
4. Can you ask for and give a description of something? (p. 58)	• How would you ask someone to describe something? • How would you describe something?

¿Qué te gusta hacer?

Geocultura
- [ ] Read and study the information on Texas in **Geocultura,** pp. 76–79.

Vocabulario 1
- [ ] Study the words and expressions in **Vocabulario 1,** pp. 82–83, and in **Más vocabulario,** p. 82, to learn to talk about what you and others like to do.
- [ ] Write the expressions from pp. 82–83 on index cards, and on the back of each card make a small drawing to help you remember the expression on the front (a skate, a basketball, etc.).
- [ ] Study the expressions in **Más vocabulario,** p. 83, to learn how to say with whom things can be done.
- [ ] Study the expressions in **¡Exprésate!,** p. 83, to learn how to ask and answer questions about what others like to do.
- [ ] Read about school sports in Latin American countries in **Nota cultural,** p. 84.
- [ ] Use the online textbook to do listening Activity 1, p. 84.
- [ ] Do Activities 2–3, p. 84, in writing.
- [ ] Study the expressions in **¡Exprésate!,** p. 85, to learn how to ask what a friend wants to do and how to answer if you are asked.
- [ ] Write out Activities 4–5, p. 85.
- [ ] For additional practice with **Vocabulario 1,** do the activities on pp. 25–27 in the *Cuaderno de vocabulario y gramática.*

Gramática 1
- [ ] Study the presentation on **gustar** with infinitives, p. 86, and read **En inglés,** p. 86.
- [ ] Write out Activities 7–9, pp. 86–87.
- [ ] Study the presentation on pronouns after prepositions, p. 88, and read **¿Te acuerdas?,** p. 88.
- [ ] Do Activities 11–13, pp. 88–89, in writing.
- [ ] Read about friendship in Latin America in **Nota cultural,** p. 90.
- [ ] Study the presentation on the present tense of **querer** with infinitives, p. 90.
- [ ] Do Activities 15–17, pp. 90–91, in writing.
- [ ] Use the online textbook to do listening Activity 18, p. 91.
- [ ] For additional practice with **Gramática 1,** do the activities on pp. 28–30 in the *Cuaderno de vocabulario y gramática* and on pp. 21–23 in the *Cuaderno de actividades.*

CHAPTER CHECKLIST

Vocabulario 2

☐ Study the words and expressions in **Vocabulario 2,** pp. 94–95, and **Más vocabulario,** p. 95, to learn how to talk about everyday activities and say where you go.

☐ Write the expressions on pp. 94–95 on index cards, and on the back of each card make a small drawing to help you remember the expression on the front (a telephone, piano keys, etc.).

☐ Study the expressions in **¡Exprésate!,** p. 95, to learn how to ask and tell about everyday activities.

☐ Read about who pays when friends go out together in **Nota cultural,** p. 96.

☐ Do Activities 20–21, p. 96, in writing.

☐ Study the expressions in **¡Exprésate!,** p. 96, to learn how to ask and say how often you and others do things.

☐ Study **Más vocabulario,** p. 97, to learn how to say how often and on which days you do things.

☐ Do Activities 22–23, p. 97, in writing.

☐ Use the online textbook to do listening Activity 24, p. 97.

☐ For additional practice with **Vocabulario 2,** do the activities on pp. 31–33 in the *Cuaderno de vocabulario y gramática.*

Gramática 2

☐ Study the presentation on the present tense of regular **-ar** verbs and read **En inglés,** p. 98.

☐ Write out Activities 26–28, pp. 98–99.

☐ Study the presentation on the present tense of **ir** and **jugar,** p. 100, and read **¿Te acuerdas?,** p. 100.

☐ Do Activities 30–32, pp. 100–101, in writing.

☐ Study the presentation on weather expressions, p. 102.

☐ Do Activity 34, p. 102, in writing.

☐ Use the online textbook to do listening Activity 35, p. 103.

☐ Write out Activity 36, p. 103.

☐ For additional practice with **Gramática 2,** do the activities on pp. 34–36 in the *Cuaderno de vocabulario y gramática* and on pp. 25–27 in the *Cuaderno de actividades.*

¿Qué te gusta hacer?

1. Can you ask what others like to do? (p. 83)	• How would you ask a classmate what he or she likes to do? • How would you ask your classmate what other friends like to do?
2. Can you tell what you and others like to do and with whom? (p. 83)	• How would you tell a classmate that you like to play tennis with your friends? • How would you say that your friend likes to go bike riding?
3. Can you ask what a friend wants to do and tell what you want to do? (p. 85)	• How would you ask a classmate if he or she wants to play chess with you? • How would you say that you don't want to watch television today?
4. Can you ask about everyday activities? (p. 95)	• How would you ask a classmate what he or she does on weekends? • How would you ask your classmate what another friend does?
5. Can you respond to questions about everyday activities? (p. 95)	• How would you tell a classmate that you go to the gym on Saturdays? • How would you say that another friend doesn't go anywhere? • How would you say that you don't go to the park when the weather is bad?
6. Can you ask and answer how often? (p. 96)	• How would you ask a classmate how often he or she goes to the gym? • How would you say you almost never go to the park? • How would you say that you almost always go to soccer practice after classes?

La vida escolar

CAPÍTULO

4

CHAPTER CHECKLIST

Geocultura
☐ Read and study the information on Costa Rica in **Geocultura,** pp. 114–117.

Vocabulario 1
☐ Study the words and expressions in **Vocabulario 1,** pp. 120–121, and in **Más vocabulario,** p. 121, to learn school supplies and subjects.

☐ Study the expressions in **¡Exprésate!,** p. 121, to learn how to ask what others have or need and to tell what you have or need.

☐ Use the online textbook to do listening Activity 1, p. 122.

☐ Do Activities 2–3, p. 122, in writing.

☐ Read about different school calendars in **Nota cultural,** p. 122.

☐ Study the expressions in **¡Exprésate!,** p. 122, to learn how to ask and talk about classes.

☐ Read about high schools in Costa Rica in **Nota cultural,** p. 123.

☐ Write out Activities 4–5, p. 123.

☐ For additional practice with **Vocabulario 1,** do the activities on pp. 37–39 in the *Cuaderno de vocabulario y gramática.*

Gramática 1
☐ Study the presentation on indefinite articles, **¿cuánto?, mucho,** and **poco,** and read **En inglés,** p. 124.

☐ Do Activities 7–9, pp. 124–125, in writing.

☐ Use the online textbook to do listening Activity 10, p. 125.

☐ Study the presentation on the present tense of **tener** and some **tener** idioms, and read **En inglés,** p. 126.

☐ Use the online textbook to do listening Activity 12, p. 126.

☐ Write out Activities 13–14, p. 127.

☐ Study the presentation on the verb **venir** and **a** + time, p. 128.

☐ Use the online textbook to do listening Activity 16, p. 128.

☐ Do Activities 17–18, pp. 128–129, in writing.

☐ For additional practice with **Gramática 1,** do the activities on pp. 40–42 in the *Cuaderno de vocabulario y gramática* and on pp. 31–33 in the *Cuaderno de actividades.*

    10

CHAPTER CHECKLIST

Vocabulario 2

☐ Study the words and expressions in **Vocabulario 2,** pp. 132–133, to talk about events and when they happen.

☐ Study the expressions in **¡Exprésate!,** p. 133, to learn how to ask and talk about plans.

☐ Read about passing and failing in **Nota cultural,** p. 134.

☐ Use the online textbook to do listening Activity 20, p. 134.

☐ Do Activities 21–22, p. 134, in writing.

☐ Study the expressions in **¡Exprésate!,** p. 134, to learn how to invite a friend to do something and how to respond to an invitation.

☐ Use the online textbook to do listening Activity 23, p. 135.

☐ Write out Activities 24–25, p. 135.

☐ For additional practice with **Vocabulario 2,** do the activities on pp. 43–45 in the *Cuaderno de vocabulario y gramática.*

Gramática 2

☐ Study the presentation on **ir a** with infinitives and read **¿Te acuerdas?,** p. 136.

☐ Use the online textbook to do listening Activity 27, p. 136.

☐ Do Activities 28–30, pp. 136–137, in writing.

☐ Study the presentation on the present tense of **-er** and **-ir** verbs and tag questions, p. 138.

☐ Read about school schedules in **Nota cultural,** p. 138.

☐ Do Activities 32–34, pp. 138–139, in writing.

☐ Study the presentation on some **-er/-ir** verbs with irregular **yo** forms, p. 140.

☐ Write out Activities 36–38, pp. 140–141.

☐ For additional practice with **Gramática 2,** do the activities on pp. 46–48 in the *Cuaderno de vocabulario y gramática* and on pp. 35–37 in the *Cuaderno de actividades.*

La vida escolar

1. Can you ask someone what he or she has? (p. 121)	• How would you ask a classmate if he/she has some folders?
2. Can you ask someone what he or she needs? (p. 121)	• How would you ask a classmate if he/she needs a bookbag?
3. Can you say what you have or need? (p. 121)	• How would you say you need a dictionary for Spanish class? • How would you say you have a ton of pencils?
4. Can you ask someone about his or her classes and tell about yours? (p. 122)	• How would you ask a classmate what his/her favorite subject is? • How would you tell which classes you have this afternoon?
5. Can you ask and talk about plans? (p. 133)	• How would you ask a classmate what he or she is going to do next Saturday? • How would you say that you're going to go to the mall in the afternoon?
6. Can you invite a friend to do something? (p. 134)	• How would you ask a friend to go with you to a soccer game? • How would you check that a friend is coming with you to the cafeteria?
7. Can you respond to invitations? (p. 134)	• How would you say "yes, of course"? • How would you say that you're not going because you have to study?

En casa con la familia

Geocultura

☐ Read and study the information on Chile in **Geocultura,** pp. 152–155.

Vocabulario 1

☐ Study the words and expressions in **Vocabulario 1,** pp. 158–159 and in **Más vocabulario,** p. 159 to learn vocabulary for family relationships and ways of describing people.

☐ Study the expressions in **¡Exprésate!,** p. 159, to learn how to ask and respond about people and family relationships.

☐ Read about Hispanic surnames in **Nota cultural,** p. 160.

☐ Use the online textbook to do listening Activity 1, p. 160.

☐ Write out Activities 2–5, pp. 160–161.

☐ For additional practice with **Vocabulario 1,** do the activities on pp. 49–51 in the *Cuaderno de vocabulario y gramática.*

Gramática 1

☐ Study the presentation on possessive adjectives, and read **En inglés,** p. 162.

☐ Write out Activity 7, p. 162.

☐ Read about elderly people in Spanish-speaking countries in **Nota cultural,** p. 163.

☐ Use the online textbook to do listening Activity 8, p. 163.

☐ Write out Activity 9, p. 163.

☐ Study the presentation on stem-changing verbs: **o —> ue,** and read **¿Te acuerdas?,** p. 164.

☐ Write out Activities 11–12, pp. 164–165.

☐ Study the presentation on stem-changing verbs: **e —> ie,** and read **¿Te acuerdas?,** p. 166.

☐ Write out Activity 14, p. 166.

☐ Do Activity 15, p. 167, in writing.

☐ For additional practice with **Gramática 1,** do the activities on pp. 52–54 in the *Cuaderno de vocabulario y gramática* and on pp. 41–43 in the *Cuaderno de actividades.*

13

CHAPTER CHECKLIST

Vocabulario 2

☐ Study the words and expressions in **Vocabulario 2,** pp. 170–171 to learn about parts of the house and locations.

☐ Study the expressions in **¡Exprésate!,** p. 171, to learn how to ask others to describe where they live and how to describe where you live.

☐ Write out Activities 17–18, p. 172.

☐ Study the expressions in **¡Exprésate!,** p. 172, to learn how to ask and respond about responsibilities.

☐ Use the online textbook to do listening Activity 19, p. 173.

☐ Write out Activities 20–21, p. 173.

☐ For additional practice with **Vocabulario 2,** do the activities on pp. 55–57 in the *Cuaderno de vocabulario y gramática.*

Gramática 2

☐ Study the presentation on **estar** with prepositions, p. 174.

☐ Read about housing styles in **Nota cultural,** p. 174.

☐ Do Activities 23–25, pp. 174–175, in writing.

☐ Study the presentation on negation with **nunca, tampoco, nadie,** and **nada,** and read **¿Te acuerdas?,** p. 176.

☐ Use the online textbook to do listening Activity 27, p. 176.

☐ Write out Activities 28–29, p. 177.

☐ Study the presentation on **tocar** and **parecer,** and read **¿Te acuerdas?,** p. 178.

☐ Use the online textbook to do listening Activity 31, p. 178.

☐ Write out Activities 32–33, p. 179.

☐ For additional practice with **Gramática 2,** do the activities on pp. 58–60 in the *Cuaderno de vocabulario y gramática* and on pp. 45–47 in the *Cuaderno de actividades.*

(14)

En casa con la familia

---

1. Can you ask about people and family relationships? (p. 159)

- How would you ask a classmate how many people are in his/her family?
- How would you ask a friend what his/her parents are like?

---

2. Can you describe people and tell about family relationships? (p. 159)

- How would you say that your parents have brown hair and wear glasses?
- How would you say that your grandfather is tall and thin, that he has gray hair, and that he has five grandchildren?

---

3. Can you ask others to describe where they live? (p. 171)

- How would you ask a friend where he/she lives?
- How would you ask a classmate what his/her house is like?

---

4. Can you describe where you live? (p. 171)

- How would you say that you live in an apartment in a small four-story building?
- How would you say the apartment has three bedrooms, two baths, a living room, and a kitchen?

---

5. Can you ask and tell about responsibilities? (p. 172)

- How would you ask a classmate what he/she thinks about helping out at home?
- How would you say that your mom almost always cleans the kitchen?
- How would you say you have to cut the grass?
- How would you say that your sister never has to clean the bathroom and it seems unfair to you?

CAPÍTULO

¡A comer!

CHAPTER CHECKLIST

Geocultura
☐ Read and study the information on Mexico in **Geocultura,** pp. 190–193.

Vocabulario 1
☐ Study the words in **Vocabulario 1,** pp. 196–197, and the expressions in **Exprésate,** p. 197, to learn how to comment on food.

☐ Read about traditional foods in **Nota cultural,** p. 198.

☐ Do Activities 1 and 3, p. 198, in writing.

☐ Use the online textbook to do listening Activity 2, p. 198.

☐ Study the expressions in **¡Exprésate!,** p. 198, to learn how to take someone's order and request something.

☐ Write out Activities 4–5, p. 199.

☐ For additional practice with **Vocabulario 1,** do the activities on pp. 61–63 in the *Cuaderno de vocabulario y gramática.*

Gramática 1
☐ Study the presentation on **ser** and **estar,** p. 200.

☐ Read about corn in **Nota cultural,** p. 200.

☐ Do Activities 7–10, pp. 200–201, in writing.

☐ Study the presentation on **pedir** and **servir,** and read **¿Te acuerdas?,** p. 202.

☐ Use the online textbook to do listening Activity 12, p. 202.

☐ Write out Activities 13–15, pp. 202–203.

☐ Study the presentation on **preferir, poder,** and **probar,** and read **¿Te acuerdas?,** p. 204.

☐ Do Activities 17–19, pp. 204–205, in writing.

☐ For additional practice with **Gramática 1,** do the activities on pp. 64–66 in the *Cuaderno de vocabulario y gramática* and on pp. 51–53 in the *Cuaderno de actividades.*

CHAPTER CHECKLIST

Vocabulario 2

☐ Study the words in **Vocabulario 2,** pp. 208–209, to learn more food vocabulary.

☐ Study the expressions in **¡Exprésate!,** p. 209, to learn how to talk about meals.

☐ Read about meals in different Spanish-speaking countries in **Nota cultural,** p. 210.

☐ Do Activities 21–23, p. 210, in writing.

☐ Study the expressions in **¡Exprésate!,** p. 211, to learn how to offer help and give instructions.

☐ Use the online textbook to do listening Activity 24, p. 211.

☐ For additional practice with **Vocabulario 2,** do the activities on pp. 67–69 in the *Cuaderno de vocabulario y gramática.*

Gramática 2

☐ Study the presentation on direct objects and direct object pronouns, and read **¿Te acuerdas?,** p. 212.

☐ Do Activities 26–28, pp. 212–213, in writing.

☐ Study the presentation on affirmative informal commands, p. 214.

☐ Read about snacks in **Nota cultural,** p. 214.

☐ Do Activities 30–31, pp. 214–215, in writing.

☐ Study the presentation on affirmative informal commands with pronouns, p. 216.

☐ Write out Activities 34–35, p. 216.

☐ Use the online textbook to do listening Activity 36, p. 217.

☐ Do Activity 37, p. 217.

☐ For additional practice with **Gramática 2,** do the activities on pp. 70–72 in the *Cuaderno de vocabulario y gramática* and on pp. 55–57 in the *Cuaderno de actividades.*

17

¡A comer!

1. Can you comment on food? (p. 197)	• How would you ask a classmate how the ham and cheese sandwich is? • How would you say they make very good fruit salad here? • How would you say that you never order salads, that you don't like them?
2. Can you make polite requests? (p. 198)	• How would you ask a classmate what he/she would like? • How would you say that you would like a tuna sandwich? • How would you say that you want orange juice to drink?
3. Can you talk about meals? (p. 209)	• How would you say that you always have toast and hot chocolate for breakfast? • How would you ask what's for lunch? • How would you say we're going to have chicken and carrots?
4. Can you offer help? (p. 211)	• How would you ask a classmate if he/she needs help?
5. Can you give instructions? (p. 211)	• How would you tell a classmate to get the cake out of the refrigerator? • How would you tell your brother to set the table?

(18)

CAPÍTULO
7

Cuerpo sano, mente sana

CHAPTER CHECKLIST

Geocultura

☐ Read and study the information on Argentina in **Geocultura,** pp. 228–231.

Vocabulario 1

☐ Study the words and expressions in **Vocabulario 1,** pp. 234–235, to learn to talk about a daily routine.

☐ Study the expressions in **¡Exprésate!,** p. 235, to learn how to talk about your daily routine.

☐ Read about skiing in Argentina in **Nota cultural,** p. 236.

☐ Write out Activities 1–3, p. 236.

☐ Study the expressions in **¡Exprésate!,** p. 237, to learn how to talk about staying fit and healthy.

☐ Use the online textbook to do listening Activity 4, p. 237.

☐ Write out Activity 5, p. 237.

☐ For additional practice with **Vocabulario 1,** do the activities on pp. 73–75 in the *Cuaderno de vocabulario y gramática.*

Gramática 1

☐ Study the presentation on verbs with reflexive pronouns, p. 238.

☐ Use the online textbook to do listening Activity 7, p. 238.

☐ Write out Activities 8–9, p. 239.

☐ Study the presentation on using infinitives, and read **En inglés,** p. 240.

☐ Write out Activities 11–13, pp. 240–241.

☐ Study the presentation on stem-changing verbs, and read **¿Te acuerdas?,** p. 242.

☐ Use the online textbook to do listening Activity 16, p. 242.

☐ Write out Activities 17–19, pp. 242–243.

☐ For additional practice with **Gramática 1,** do the activities on pp. 76–78 in the *Cuaderno de vocabulario y gramática* and on pp. 61–63 in the *Cuaderno de actividades.*

(19)

CHAPTER CHECKLIST

Vocabulario 2

☐ Study the words and expressions in **Vocabulario 2,** pp. 246–247, and in **Más vocabulario,** p. 247, to learn vocabulary for parts of the body, feelings, and health.

☐ Study the expressions in **¡Exprésate!,** p. 247, to learn how to ask how someone feels and to say how you feel.

☐ Read about Argentine cooking in **Nota cultural,** p. 248.

☐ Write out Activities 21–22, p. 248.

☐ Study the expressions in **¡Exprésate!,** p. 248, to learn how to give advice.

☐ Read about an Argentine herbal tea in **Nota cultural,** p. 249.

☐ Use the online textbook to do listening Activity 23, p. 249.

☐ Write out Activity 24, p. 249.

☐ For additional practice with **Vocabulario 2,** do the activities on pp. 79–81 in the *Cuaderno de vocabulario y gramática.*

Gramática 2

☐ Study the presentation on **estar, sentirse,** and **tener,** p. 250.

☐ Use the online textbook to do listening Activity 26, p. 250.

☐ Write out Activities 27–28, p. 251.

☐ Study the presentation on negative informal commands, and read **¿Te acuerdas?,** p. 252.

☐ Write out Activities 30–32, pp. 252–253.

☐ Study the presentation on object and reflexive pronouns with commands, and read **¿Te acuerdas?,** p. 254.

☐ Write out Activities 34–36, pp. 254–255.

☐ For additional practice with **Gramática 2,** do the activities on pp. 82–84 in the *Cuaderno de vocabulario y gramática* and on pp. 65–67 in the *Cuaderno de actividades.*

Cuerpo sano, mente sana

1. Can you talk about your daily routine? (p. 235)

- How would you ask a classmate what he/she still has to do?
- How would you say you have to eat breakfast and then brush your teeth?
- How would you say that you have to shave, but you can't find the razor?

2. Can you talk about staying fit and healthy? (p. 237)

- How would you ask a classmate what he/she does to stay in shape?
- How would you say that you stretch before running?
- How would you ask a friend what he/she does to relax?
- How would you say that to relax you like to listen to music?

3. Can you ask how someone feels? (p. 247)

- How would you ask a friend what's wrong with him/her?
- How would you ask a classmate what's the matter with another classmate?

4. Can you say how you feel or how someone else feels? (p. 247)

- How would you say you feel a little nervous and your head hurts?
- How would you say a classmate is tired and his/her legs hurt?

5. Can you give advice? (p. 248)

- How would you tell a classmate that he/she should do yoga to relax?
- How would you tell a classmate to do exercise?
- How would you tell a classmate to go to bed earlier?

Vamos de compras

Geocultura

☐ Read and study the information on Florida in **Geocultura,** pp. 266–269.

Vocabulario 1

☐ Study the words and expressions in **Vocabulario 1,** pp. 272–273, and in **Más vocabulario,** p. 272, to learn articles of clothing and types of fabric.

☐ Study the expressions in ¡**Exprésate!,** p. 273, to learn how to ask for an opinion and give your opinion.

☐ Read about metric system sizes in **Nota cultural,** p. 274.

☐ Use the online textbook to do listening Activity 1, p. 274.

☐ Do Activities 2–3, p. 274, in writing.

☐ Study the expressions in ¡**Exprésate!,** p. 275, to learn how to offer and ask for help in a store.

☐ For additional practice with **Vocabulario 1,** do the activities on pp. 85–87 in the *Cuaderno de vocabulario y gramática.*

Gramática 1

☐ Study the presentation on **costar** and numbers to 1 million, p. 276.

☐ Use the online textbook to do listening Activity 6, p. 276.

☐ Do Activities 7–8, p. 277, in writing.

☐ Study the presentation on demonstrative adjectives and comparisons, p. 278.

☐ Read about a special Cuban shirt in **Nota cultural,** p. 278.

☐ Use the online textbook to do listening Activity 10, p. 278.

☐ Write out Activities 11–12, p. 279.

☐ Study the presentation on **quedar,** and read ¿**Te acuerdas?,** p. 280.

☐ Do Activity 14, p. 280, in writing.

☐ Use the online textbook to do listening Activity 15, p. 281.

☐ Do Activity 16, p. 281, in writing.

☐ For additional practice with **Gramática 1,** do the activities on pp. 88–90 in the *Cuaderno de vocabulario y gramática* and on pp. 71–73 in the *Cuaderno de actividades.*

CHAPTER CHECKLIST

Vocabulario 2

☐ Study the words and expressions in **Vocabulario 2,** pp. 284–285, and in **Más vocabulario,** p. 285, to learn vocabulary for stores and shopping.

☐ Study the expressions in **¡Exprésate!,** p. 285, to learn how to ask and respond about where someone went and what someone did.

☐ Read about Spanish-speaking consumers in the United States in **Nota cultural,** p. 286.

☐ Do Activities 18 and 20, p. 286, in writing.

☐ Use the online textbook to do listening Activity 19, p. 286.

☐ Study the expressions in **¡Exprésate!,** p. 287, to learn how to talk on the phone.

☐ Write out Activity 21, p. 287.

☐ For additional practice with **Vocabulario 2,** do the activities on pp. 91–93 in the *Cuaderno de vocabulario y gramática.*

Gramática 2

☐ Study the presentation on the preterite of **-ar** verbs, p. 288.

☐ Read about bargaining in **Nota cultural,** p. 288.

☐ Use the online textbook to do listening Activity 23, p. 288.

☐ Do Activities 24–25, pp. 288–289, in writing.

☐ Study the presentation on the preterite of **ir,** p. 290.

☐ Write out Activity 27, p. 290.

☐ Do Activities 28–29, pp. 290–291, in writing.

☐ Study the review of the preterite of **-ar** verbs with reflexive pronouns, p. 292.

☐ Use the online textbook to do listening Activity 31, p. 292.

☐ Write out Activities 32–33, p. 293.

☐ For additional practice with **Gramática 2,** do the activities on pp. 94–96 in the *Cuaderno de vocabulario y gramática* and on pp. 75–77 in the *Cuaderno de actividades.*

23

Vamos de compras

1. Can you describe what you are wearing? (p. 273)	• How would you say you're wearing jeans, a yellow shirt, sneakers, and white socks?
2. Can you ask for someone's opinion? (p. 273)	• How would you ask a classmate what he/she thinks of a shirt? • How would you ask how a pair of pants fits you?
3. Can you give your opinion? (p. 273)	• How would you say that something looks good on your friend? • How would you say that the pants are too expensive?
4. Can you offer and ask for help in a store? (p. 275)	• How would you ask a customer how you can help him/her? • How would you say that you need a smaller size?
5. Can you ask where someone went and what someone did? (p. 285)	• How would you ask a classmate where he/she went and what he/she did last weekend?
6. Can you tell where you went and what you did? (p. 285)	• How would you say that you went to the mall and bought some ear-phones?
7. Can you talk on the phone? (p. 287)	• How would you ask who's calling? • How would you say that you'll call back later?

¡Festejemos!

Geocultura

☐ Read and study the information on the Dominican Republic in **Geocultura,** pp. 304–307.

Vocabulario 1

☐ Study the words and expressions in **Vocabulario 1,** pp. 310–311, and in **Más vocabulario,** p. 311, to learn names of holidays and ways to observe them.

☐ Study the expressions in **¡Exprésate!,** p. 311, to learn how to ask about someone's plans and to respond to questions about your own plans.

☐ Do Activities 1–2, p. 312, in writing.

☐ Study the expressions in **¡Exprésate!,** p. 312, to learn how to ask and respond about past holidays.

☐ Read about Dominican Independence Day in **Nota cultural,** p. 313.

☐ Write out Activities 3 and 5, p. 313.

☐ Use the online textbook to do listening Activity 4, p. 313.

☐ For additional practice with **Vocabulario 1,** do the activities on pp. 97–99 in the *Cuaderno de vocabulario y gramática.*

Gramática 1

☐ Study the presentation on the preterite of **-er** and **-ir** verbs, and read **¿Te acuerdas?,** p. 314.

☐ Write out Activities 7–9, pp. 314–315.

☐ Study the review of the preterite, and read **¿Te acuerdas?,** p. 316.

☐ Use the online textbook to do listening Activity 12, p. 316.

☐ Do Activities 13–15, pp. 316–317, in writing.

☐ Study the presentation on **pensar que** and **pensar** with infinitives, p. 318.

☐ Read about a Dominican Christmas dish in **Nota Cultural,** p. 318.

☐ Write out Activities 17–18, pp. 318–319.

☐ For additional practice with **Gramática 1,** do the activities on pp. 100–102 in the *Cuaderno de vocabulario y gramática* and on pp. 81–83 in the *Cuaderno de actividades.*

CHAPTER CHECKLIST

Vocabulario 2

☐ Study the words and expressions in **Vocabulario 2,** pp. 322–323, and **Más vocabulario,** p. 323, to learn vocabulary for party preparations.

☐ Study the expressions in **¡Exprésate!,** p. 323, to learn how to ask and respond to questions about preparing for a party.

☐ Read about **la quinceañera** in **Nota cultural,** p. 324.

☐ Do Activities 20–21, p. 324, in writing.

☐ Study the expressions in **¡Exprésate!,** p. 325, to learn how to greet, introduce others, and say goodbye.

☐ Use the online textbook to do listening Activity 22, p. 325.

☐ Write out Activity 23, p. 325.

☐ For additional practice with **Vocabulario 2,** do the activities on pp. 103–105 in the *Cuaderno de vocabulario y gramática.*

Gramática 2

☐ Study the presentation on direct object pronouns, and read **¿Te acuerdas?,** p. 326.

☐ Write out Activities 25–27, pp. 326–327.

☐ Read about dancing at parties in **Nota cultural,** p. 327.

☐ Study the presentation on **conocer** and personal **a,** p. 328.

☐ Write out Activity 29, p. 328.

☐ Do Activities 30–31, p. 329, in writing.

☐ Study the presentation on the present progressive, p. 330.

☐ Use the online textbook to do listening Activity 33, p. 330.

☐ Write out Activity 34, p. 331.

☐ For additional practice with **Gramática 2,** do the activities on pp. 106–108 in the *Cuaderno de vocabulario y gramática* and on pp. 85–87 in the *Cuaderno de actividades.*

(26)

¡Festejemos!

<table>
<tr>
<td>

1. Can you ask about someone's plans for a holiday and tell about your plans? (p. 311)

</td>
<td>

• How would you ask a classmate what he/she is going to do on Valentine's Day?

• How would you ask a group of friends what they have planned for New Year's Eve?

• How would you say that you plan to to spend Christmas Eve with your grandparents?

</td>
</tr>
<tr>
<td>

2. Can you ask and tell about past holidays? (p. 312)

</td>
<td>

• How would ask a classmate where he or she spent Thanksgiving last year?

• How would you say that you spent a holiday at home?

</td>
</tr>
<tr>
<td>

3. Can you ask and answer questions about preparing for a party? (p. 323)

</td>
<td>

• How would you ask a classmate if everything is ready for the party?

• How would you ask a classmate if he/she finished the preparations already?

• How would you say that people are hanging the decorations now?

</td>
</tr>
<tr>
<td>

4. Can you greet, introduce others, and say good-bye? (p. 325)

</td>
<td>

• How would you tell a classmate that it's great to see him/her?

• How would you introduce your parents to a classmate?

• How would you tell someone that it's nice to meet him/her?

• How would you tell a classmate goodbye and that you'll call him/her later?

</td>
</tr>
</table>

27

¡A viajar!

Geocultura

☐ Read and study the information on Peru in **Geocultura,** pp. 342–345.

Vocabulario 1

☐ Study the words in **Vocabulario 1,** pp. 348–349, and in **Más vocabulario,** p. 349, to learn travel vocabulary.

☐ Study the expressions in **¡Exprésate!,** p. 349, to learn how to ask for and give information.

☐ Read about the Uros Islands in **Nota cultural,** p. 350.

☐ Use the online textbook to do listening Activity 1, p. 350.

☐ Do Activities 2–3, p. 350, in writing.

☐ Study the expressions in **¡Exprésate!,** p. 351, to learn how to remind and reassure.

☐ Write out Activity 4, p. 351.

☐ For additional practice with **Vocabulario 1,** do the activities on pp. 109–111 in the *Cuaderno de vocabulario y gramática.*

Gramática 1

☐ Study the review of the preterite, and read **¿Te acuerdas?,** p. 352.

☐ Use the online textbook to do listening Activity 7, p. 352.

☐ Do Activity 8, p. 353, in writing.

☐ Study the presentation on the preterite of **-car, -gar, -zar** verbs, p. 354.

☐ Use the online textbook to do listening Activity 10, p. 354.

☐ Do Activities 11–12, pp. 354–355, in writing.

☐ Study the presentation on the preterite of **hacer,** p. 356.

☐ Read about Incan grain in **Nota cultural,** p. 356.

☐ Do Activities 14–15, p. 356, in writing.

☐ For additional practice with **Gramática 1,** do the activities on pp. 112–114 in the *Cuaderno de vocabulario y gramática* and on pp. 91–93 in the *Cuaderno de actividades.*

CHAPTER CHECKLIST

Vocabulario 2

☐ Study the words and expressions in **Vocabulario 2,** pp. 360–361 and in **Más vocabulario,** p. 361, to learn vocabulary related to vacations and transportation.

☐ Study the expressions in **¡Exprésate!,** p. 361, to learn how to talk about a trip.

☐ Read about train travel in Peru in **Nota cultural,** p. 362.

☐ Use the online textbook to do listening Activity 18, p. 362.

☐ Do Activities 19–20, p. 362, in writing.

☐ Study the expressions in **¡Exprésate!,** p. 363, to learn how to express hopes and wishes.

☐ Do Activity 21, p. 363, in writing.

☐ For additional practice with **Vocabulario 2,** do the activities on pp. 115–117 in the *Cuaderno de vocabulario y gramática.*

Gramática 2

☐ Study the presentation on informal commands of spelling-change and irregular verbs, and read **¿Te acuerdas?,** p. 364.

☐ Use the online textbook to do listening Activity 24, p. 365.

☐ Do Activity 25, p. 365, in writing.

☐ Study the review of direct object pronouns, and read **¿Te acuerdas?,** p. 366.

☐ Use the online textbook to do listening Activity 27, p. 366.

☐ Do Activities 28–30, pp. 366–367, in writing.

☐ Study the review of verbs followed by infinitives, p. 368.

☐ Do Activities 32–34, pp. 368–369, in writing.

☐ For additional practice with **Gramática 2,** do the activities on pp. 118–120 in the *Cuaderno de vocabulario y gramática* and on pp. 95–97 in the *Cuaderno de actividades.*

(29)

¡A viajar!

1. Can you ask for and give information? (p. 349)	• How would you ask a stranger if he/she can tell you where the baggage claim is? • How would you say the waiting room is around the corner? • How would you ask a stranger if he/she knows where you can get a boarding pass?
2. Can you remind someone of something? (p. 351)	• How would you ask a friend if he/she found his/her passport already? • How would you ask a friend if he/she already packed his/her suitcases?
3. Can you reassure someone about something? (p. 351)	• How would you tell a friend not to worry, that he/she can buy a book at the airport?
4. Can you talk about a trip? (p. 361)	• How would you ask how someone's trip was? • How would you ask some friends what they did? • How would you say that you toured the city by bus and took a lot of pictures?
5. Can you express hopes and wishes? (p. 363)	• How would you say that one day you would like to visit Peru? • How would you say that you hope to see the ruins of Machu Picchu?

30

Holt Spanish 1

Fold-n-Learn Project Suggestions

¡Empecemos!

FOLD-N-LEARN PROJECT SUGGESTIONS

Follow the instructions below to create a fun study aid. This aid will help you review the expressions listed on page 35 of your textbook.

MATERIALS You will need lined paper and a pen or pencil.

STEP 1 Fold a sheet of paper into thirds from top to bottom.

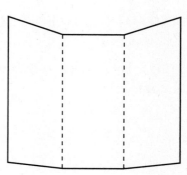

STEP 2 Unfold the paper. At the top of the middle column of the page, write the first category name on page 35 of your book: Asking someone's name and saying yours. Then write the Spanish expressions for asking someone's name and saying yours underneath the category name.

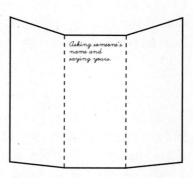

STEP 3 Copy the Spanish expressions for the other categories in the same way, keeping them all in the middle column. Use as many pages as you need.

STEP 4 Write the English equivalent for each Spanish expression in the left-hand column of the page so that you can see the English phrases on the left and the Spanish phrases in the middle.

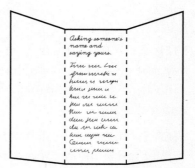

STEP 5 Fold the part of the page that makes the right column along the fold line you made for Step 1 so that the right third of the page covers the middle.

STEP 6 Review the chapter expressions with the pages you've created. Read each English expression on the left while you try to come up with its Spanish equivalent hidden in the middle.

    33

A conocernos

FOLD-N-LEARN PROJECT SUGGESTIONS

Follow the instructions below to create a fun study aid. This aid will help you review the expressions listed on page 73 of your textbook.

MATERIALS You will need lined paper, scissors, and a pen or pencil.

STEP 1 Fold a sheet of paper in half from top to bottom.

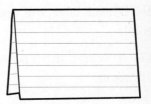

STEP 2 Now fold the sheet of paper in half from side to side. Unfold the sheet so that you see the two sections formed by the crease of the first fold.

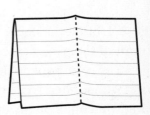

STEP 3 Starting at the top of the sheet of paper, cut along the top-to-bottom fold as far as the fold in the middle of the sheet to form two flaps.

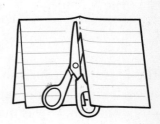

STEP 4 On the left flap, write Spanish words to describe guys and masculine nouns. Write the English equivalent for each Spanish expression in the section under the flap.

STEP 5 On the right flap, write words to describe girls and feminine nouns. Write the English equivalent in the section underneath. Use as many sheets as you need.

STEP 6 Review the chapter descriptive words with the flip charts you've created. Read each Spanish word on the flaps while you try to remember the English equivalent hidden underneath.

34

¿Qué te gusta hacer?

FOLD-N-LEARN PROJECT SUGGESTIONS

Follow the instructions below to create a fun study aid. This aid will help you review many of the expressions listed on page 111 of your textbook.

MATERIALS You will need a sheet of unlined paper, glue or tape, and a pen or pencil.

STEP 1 Fold a 2-inch lengthwise flap in a sheet of paper.

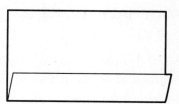

STEP 2 Now, fold a ½-inch flap on either end of the sheet of the paper. Glue or tape these flaps where they meet the original 2-inch fold.

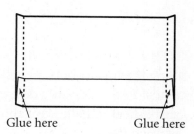

Glue here   Glue here

STEP 3 When the flaps are dry, fold the paper in half so that the two folded ends meet with the pockets on the inside. On both sides of your pocket folder, write **Chapter 3 Flashcards.**

Chapter 3 Flashcards

STEP 4 If you haven't already made them, use 3″ × 5″ index cards to create flashcards for **Vocabulario 1** and **Vocabulario 2** (see pp. 7–8 of this book), and place them in the left pocket, drawing side up.

STEP 5 Review the expressions in Chapter 3 by taking a flashcard from the file pocket, looking at the drawing, and trying to recall the expression written on the other side. If you are correct, place the card in the right pocket. If not, file the card in last place in the left pocket for further review.

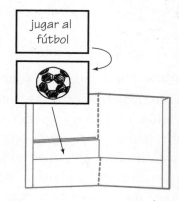

jugar al fútbol

35

La vida escolar

FOLD-N-LEARN PROJECT SUGGESTIONS

Follow the instructions below to create a fun study aid. This aid will help you review many of the verbs listed on page 149 of your textbook.

MATERIALS You will need a sheet of lined paper, a stapler or paper clips, scissors, and a pen or pencil.

STEP 1 Fold a sheet of paper in half from top to bottom, then from side to side so that the sheet is folded in fourths.

STEP 2 Unfold the sheet. Using scissors, cut a slit along the top-to-bottom crease from each edge almost to the side-to-side crease. Do not cut the entire sheet in half; leave about $\frac{1}{4}$ inch in the center between the slits.

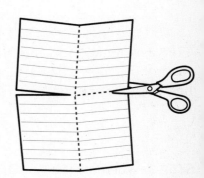

STEP 3 Fold the sheet again in fourths in the same order as Step 1 to form a four-page booklet. On the cover, write "Verb Manual."

STEP 4 On the pages of your booklet, write the conjugations of verbs from page 149, such as **tener, venir, hacer, poner, ver, saber,** and **salir.** Include the subject pronouns in the conjugations. Insert another folded and cut sheet in the center if you wish to include more verbs. Secure the pages with paper clips or staples.

STEP 5 Review the verbs in Chapter 4 by flipping through the manual and selecting a verb. Cover the verb forms and give them by looking only at the subject pronouns.

En casa con la familia

FOLD-N-LEARN PROJECT SUGGESTIONS

Follow the instructions below to create a fun study aid. This aid will help you review many of the expressions listed on page 187 of your textbook.

MATERIALS You will need a sheet of unlined paper, a marker, and a pencil.

STEP 1 Fold a sheet of paper in thirds from side to side.

STEP 2 Unfold the paper. Turn the sheet so that one of the sides faces you and you see three long horizontal sections formed by the creases.

STEP 3 You're going to make your own family tree on the sheet. With a pencil, draw circles and lines on the sheet like the ones shown here, but make the number of circles you need to match your family. Put your grandparents' circles in the top section, their children in the middle, and you, your brothers and sisters, and your cousins in the bottom section of the sheet.

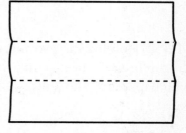

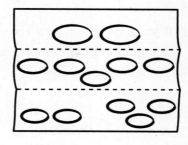

STEP 4 As you draw the circles, fill in the family tree with the real names of your family. Then trace over the lines and circles with a marker so you can see where they are through the paper. With a pencil, write each person's relationship to you in Spanish on the back of the circle he or she is in.

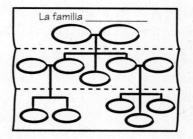

La familia _____

STEP 5 Review family relationships from page 187 with the family tree you've created. Look at the names of each person and try to come up with the relationship to you in Spanish.

CAPÍTULO
6

¡A comer!

FOLD-N-LEARN PROJECT SUGGESTIONS

Follow the instructions below to create a fun study aid. This aid will help you review the expressions listed on page 225 of your textbook.

MATERIALS You will need two sheets of paper, a stapler, and a pen or pencil.

STEP 1 Lay one sheet of paper on top of the other. Slide the top sheet up so that one inch of the bottom sheet is showing.

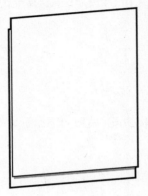

STEP 2 Holding the two sheets together, fold down the top of each sheet so that you have four one-inch flaps along the bottom.

STEP 3 Secure the layered booklet with staples. On the top, or cover page, write **¡A comer!** and beneath that **Meals and Food.**

STEP 4 On the three one-inch flaps, write **El desayuno, El almuerzo,** and **La cena.**

STEP 5 Write all the Spanish food expressions for breakfast foods on the page with **El desayuno.** Do the same for lunch and dinner foods on the other two pages. On the back of each page, write the English equivalents for the food vocabulary.

STEP 6 Review the chapter expressions with the flap booklet you've created. Read each Spanish expression on the front while you try to come up with its English equivalent on the back.

(38)

Cuerpo sano, mente sana

FOLD-N-LEARN PROJECT SUGGESTIONS

Follow the instructions below to create a fun study aid. This aid will help you review the reflexive verbs on page 262 of your textbook.

MATERIALS You will need some sheets of unlined paper and a pen or pencil.

STEP 1 Fold a sheet of paper in thirds from top to bottom.

STEP 2 Now fold the paper in half lenthwise. Open the sheet. You have a sheet divided into six horizontal sections.

STEP 3 On the left-hand side of the top section, write the infinitive form of a reflexive verb. Below that, write **singular forms.** Then, write each of the three singular conjugated verb forms in the second, fourth, and sixth sections.

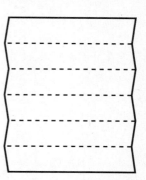

STEP 4 Turn the paper face down. Fold down the top section and write the infinitive of the verb again and below that, **plural forms.** Fold the top section back up and write the plural conjugated forms of the verb in the second, fourth, and sixth sections on this side of the page.

STEP 5 When you have finished writing the forms of the verb, follow the creases to refold the sheet in fan or accordion style. Begin by folding up the bottom section on this side of the sheet of paper.

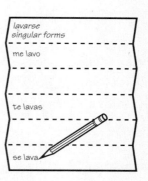

STEP 6 Review the chapter expressions by reading the infinitives on the top pleat and giving the conjugated forms of the verb. Open the pleats one by one to check your answers. Fold as many sheets as you need to conjugate all of the reflexive verbs in the chapter (one verb per sheet).

Vamos de compras

FOLD-N-LEARN PROJECT SUGGESTIONS

Follow the instructions below to create a fun study aid. This aid will help you review many of the expressions listed on page 301 of your textbook.

MATERIALS You will need a sheet of unlined paper, scissors, and a pen or pencil.

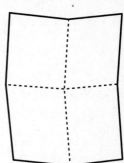

STEP 1 Fold a sheet of paper in half twice, first from side to side and then from top to bottom. Unfold the paper.

STEP 2 Turn the paper sideways. Then fold the right and left edges to meet at the center, forming two long flaps.

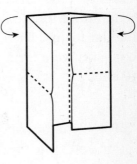

STEP 3 Using scissors, cut along the middle creases in the two long flaps to form four flaps. Do not cut past the folded edges of the long flaps.

STEP 4 On the upper left flap, write stores that are called by the long form, **la tienda de ropa,** for example. On the upper right flap, across from each store, write typical items sold there (**los pantalones**). Write the English equivalents under each upper flap.

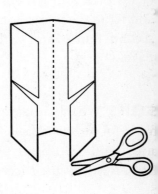

STEP 5 On the lower left flap, write stores that are called by one word, for example, **la librería.** Across from each store, on the lower right flap, write typical items sold there. Under each flap, write the English equivalents.

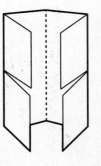

STEP 6 Review the stores and items for sale with the four-flap shopping guide you've created. Read each Spanish expression on the flaps while you try to come up with its English equivalent hidden underneath.

¡Festejemos!

FOLD-N-LEARN PROJECT SUGGESTIONS

Follow the instructions below to create a fun study aid. This aid will help you review the words and expressions listed on page 339 of your textbook.

MATERIALS You will need unlined paper and a pen or pencil.

STEP 1 Fold a sheet of paper in half by putting the top and bottom edges together.

STEP 2 Unfold the paper. Smooth the crease, and draw a line along the crease line.

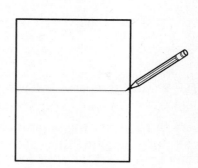

STEP 3 Fold the top and bottom edges to the marked middle crease to make a two-door entrance to expressions for holidays and celebration.

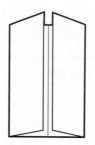

STEP 4 Choose expressions you want to review from the top half of page 339 (to talk about plans and to talk about past holidays). Write the English equivalents on the left door, and write the Spanish expressions inside, to left of the line.

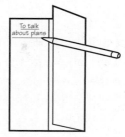

STEP 5 Do the same on the right with expressions from the bottom half of page 339 (to talk about preparing for a party and to greet, introduce others, and say good-bye). Make as many two-door sets as you need.

STEP 6 Review the chapter expressions with the doors you have created. Read each English expression on the doors while you try to come up with its Spanish equivalent inside.

¡A viajar!

FOLD-N-LEARN PROJECT SUGGESTIONS

Follow the instructions below to create a fun study aid. This aid will help you review many of the expressions listed on page 377 of your textbook.

MATERIALS You will need a sheet of lined paper, scissors, and a pen or pencil.

STEP 1 Fold a sheet of lined paper in half the long way.

STEP 2 Turn the paper sideways with the center fold away from you. Using scissors, cut along every third line in the upper half of the paper, from the edge to the fold.

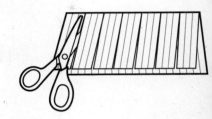

STEP 3 Turn the paper back to a vertical position. You now have a series of equal tabs for the key terms in the chapter: words and expressions related to trips.

STEP 4 Write a Spanish word or expression from page 377 on each tab. Write the English equivalent on the part of the paper underneath. Use as many sheets as you need to hold the key travel-related terms.

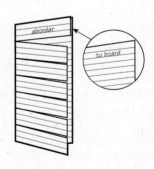

STEP 5 Review the words and expressions for trips, transportation, and vacations on page 377 with the key-term tabs you have created. Read the Spanish expression on each tab while you try to come up with its English equivalent underneath.

CARTOON NETWORK

SCOOBY-DOO! and the MARSH MONSTER

by Jesse Leon McCann

WORLDWIDE PUBLISHING™

SCHOLASTIC INC.

New York   Toronto   London   Auckland   Sydney
Mexico City   New Delhi   Hong Kong   Buenos Aires

FOR DEE AND TERI MASTERS; NIGHTS OF PUNCH,
JUDY, AND BURSTING INTO FLAME

ISBN 0-439-38211-4

Designed by Louise Bova

12 11 10 9 8 7 6 5 4 3 2 1   2 3 4 5 6 7/0

Special thanks to Duendes del Sur for
cover and interior illustrations.

Printed in the U.S.A.
First Scholastic printing, April 2002

Scooby-Doo and his pals from Mystery, Inc., were about to start their summer rafting vacation — on the river wild! They were renting equipment from Mr. Samuels, a kindly old gentleman.

The gang was all set to have a lot of fun. But then they met some unhappy river rafters who had just had a horrible experience!

The rafters introduced themselves. Their names were Jemma, Martin, and Ben.

"We were supposed to float down the river for three days, and camp on the shore of the river each night," Jemma said.

"On the second day, we were attacked by a terrible monster!" Ben exclaimed.

"Zoinks!" cried Shaggy. "A m-m-monster?!"

"R-r-ronster?" Scooby gulped.

"A big, oily monster!" exclaimed Martin. "It looked like a man, but it was covered from head to toe with something slimy and sludgy!"

"It gave an evil roar and knocked us into the water," Jemma said. "We were so scared, we hightailed it back here right away!"

"Oh, I'm so sorry this happened to you," exclaimed Mr. Samuels. "I'll give you a full refund, don't you worry!"

"We're sorry, Mr. Samuels, but we can't continue coming here if we have to worry about strange creatures attacking us," Martin said sadly. The disappointed campers packed up their car and drove away.

Just then, a pair of men who were hiking by stopped to talk to Mr. Samuels. The leader of the pair was a very rich man named Jeremiah Peabody. With him was his assistant, Hank.

"Tough luck, old sport." Peabody smiled at Mr. Samuels. "If your business is being ruined by this marsh monster, perhaps you should reconsider my offer. Sell your land to me. It might save you a lot of grief."

"Oh, no!" Mr. Samuels said sadly. "What am I going to do? I don't want to sell my land to Peabody. I just know he'll turn this place into a toxic dump for his factories!"

"Don't worry, Mr. Samuels," Fred assured him. "We'll solve this marsh monster mystery for you!"

"Like, no way, Fred!" cried Shaggy. "I'm not going near any marshes or monsters! And I'm sure not going near any marsh monsters!"

"Ree reither!" agreed Scooby, shaking his head.

But after Velma negotiated with a sack of Scooby Snacks, Shaggy and Scooby agreed to help Mr. Samuels, too.

The kids packed for their trip. Fred, Velma, and Daphne brought life jackets, a rope, helmets, and a first-aid kit. Shaggy and Scooby brought lots of food—lots and lots of food!

"I'm afraid we can't fit all that food," said Daphne. "But don't worry, guys—we'll find lots of delicious nuts and berries to eat along the way," Velma told them.

"Groovy!" Shaggy rubbed his belly. "Like, I'm just nuts over nuts and berries!"

"Reah!" Scooby licked his lips. "Ruts and rerries!"

The gang set out, coasting down the beautiful blue river, enjoying the pleasant countryside and refreshing mountain air.

But soon things started going wrong. Shaggy and Scooby kept seeing something creepy in the bushes. It seemed to be following the gang's raft! Then, as the river began to flow faster, they saw that somebody ... or something ... had torn out the sign telling them which way they should go!

"Jinkies!" Velma exclaimed. "Without that sign, we could be headed right into the rapids and we wouldn't even know it!"

The gang had two choices in picking the right fork in the river to take. Unfortunately, they picked the wrong one! Soon the river was going from calm to choppy. Big boulders appeared in the water, and the gang had to steer around them as quickly as they could.

Then the river tumbled swiftly downhill, faster and faster! There were more and more rocks in the water. They were rafting through white-water rapids.

The kids valiantly struggled to stay afloat in the churning waters.

"Zoinks!" Shaggy cried. "I feel like I'm a milk shake that's about to be blended!"

"Roh, no!" Scooby hollered as he held on for dear life.

And though the rushing river was loud, they could hear laughter. Strange, creepy laughter!

When it looked as if they'd surely tumble into the dangerous water, Daphne spotted something up ahead.

"Over there! Try and steer that direction!" Daphne was pointing to a small stream that flowed off the main river.

They dug their oars into the water and steered with all their might. After a few nervous moments, they were floating swiftly down the small stream.

"Wow, that was close!" Fred wiped the sweat from his brow.

The kids were glad they'd gotten away from the rapids safely, but they still had the strange feeling they were being followed.

"We should make camp here for the night," Fred suggested. "I want to explore this area before it's too dark. I have a feeling that whatever happened to that sign was no accident."

The gang set up camp in a dry spot in the woods. As they worked, the fog got thicker and thicker. Everything was quiet and still — until they suddenly heard footsteps crunching through leaves.

"Jeepers! Who's that?" Daphne cried as a huge figure appeared through the mists.

"Zoinks!" Shaggy bellowed. "It's the m-m-marsh m-m-monster!"

"Ruh-roh!" Scooby jumped into Shaggy's arms and held on tight. But instead of a marsh monster, it was a man—a very large man.

"I may be as big as a bear, but I'm as friendly as a puppy!" he laughed. "They call me Big Dave, and I live in this forest."

The kids were all glad Big Dave wasn't the marsh monster. They invited him to join them for dinner. When they asked him if he'd seen the marsh monster, he said he hadn't. But he did talk about another kind of villain.

"Some people are trying to wreck this forest by using it for a toxic dumping ground," Big Dave told them sadly.

"Jinkies!" Velma frowned. "It would be terrible to ruin a beautiful forest like this!"

As everyone turned in for the night, they thought carefully about what Big Dave had told them.

In the morning, Big Dave said good-bye. He even gave them a going-away present — delicious nuts and berries from the forest!

"Thanks, Big Dave!" Velma waved. "After we've solved the marsh monster mystery, we'll do everything we can to save this forest."

15

After they'd drifted down the stream a couple miles, Fred spotted a clue — something big had broken tree branches near the edge of the water.

"It could be the marsh monster," Fred said as he steered the raft ashore. "C'mon, gang, let's investigate."

Shaggy and Scooby weren't too keen on getting out of the raft. When they finally did, they insisted on taking their sacks of food with them.

"Like, there's no way I'm gonna get grabbed by a greasy ghoul on an empty stomach," Shaggy declared firmly.

"Reah, ree reither!" Scooby agreed.

The kids crept carefully past the broken branches and into the forest. After they'd gone a few hundred feet, Fred stopped suddenly.

"Did you guys hear that?" he asked.

"Like, what?" Shaggy asked nervously.

All at once, a huge form jumped out from behind a tree. It was oily. It was slimy. It was the marsh monster!

"Rrrrroooowl!" it growled fiercely.

The Mystery, Inc., gang ran as fast as they could back toward the raft.

"Zoinks!" puffed Shaggy. "Now <u>that</u> I heard, but I wish I hadn't!"

The marsh monster was fast, but the gang was faster. Well, most of them were. Scooby and Shaggy couldn't bear to part with their food, even though they were in danger. Soon they were trapped!

As the marsh monster slowly approached them, Shaggy and Scooby looked at each other with dread.

"Like, Scoob, ol' pal . . . you know what we have to do," Shaggy cried.

Scooby was sobbing. "Rye row! Rye row!"

With that they both started throwing their food at the marsh monster.

The marsh monster didn't like getting pelted with food one bit. It backed off. When they saw their chance, Shaggy and Scooby ran for it.

When they got back to the others, Velma and Daphne started dressing Shaggy and Scooby in tree and bush branches.

"Just in time!" Fred smiled. "We've got a plan and we need you guys as bait."

After the girls were done, Scooby and Shaggy were fully camouflaged in leaves.

"Like, what a day!" Shaggy exclaimed. "First we lose our food, and now we might end up as ghoulie-grub!"

"Roulie-rub?" Scooby cried. "Roh, no!"

Shaggy and Scooby ventured back into the forest, looking for the marsh monster. Covered with branches and leaves, they were able to sneak right up next to it. Shaggy tapped the creature on the shoulder.

"Like, isn't this a mahh-velous costume party?" Shaggy grinned. "My pal and I came as matching foliage. But I see you went for the garbage disposal look."

"Rrrrrowl!"

The angry marsh monster was soon chasing them through the forest again. Scooby and Shaggy climbed into the trees to stay out of its slimy clutches.

"Hey, Scooby," Shaggy called as they climbed across branches, hopping from tree to tree. "Like, you're doing pretty good! I always thought dogs couldn't climb trees!"

"Rogs ran't rimb rees?" Scooby gulped. Then he promptly fell to the ground.

"Zoinks! Like, maybe I shouldn't have said that!" cried Shaggy. He dropped down to the ground with Scooby.

The two took off running. The marsh monster was gaining on them. They could hardly keep out of the fiend's oily grasp.

Scooby-Doo and Shaggy ran toward the river, heading right to the spot that Fred had told them about. They passed Daphne, hiding behind the trunk of a tree. She signaled to Velma and Fred.

The marsh monster reached its slimy hand toward Scooby and Shaggy. It was just inches from grabbing them.

"Now!" cried Fred. He and Velma leaned on an oar they'd wedged under a big boulder. Splash! The boulder hit the water. Suddenly, the fast-moving current of the river was diverted — right at the marsh monster.

Whoooosh! The powerful rush of water knocked the monster off its slimy feet!

Fred quickly tied up the marsh monster with a rope he'd brought from the raft. When he pulled at the creature's head, Mr. Peabody's assistant, Hank, was revealed. Hank dropped a walkie-talkie from under his costume.

"I wonder who he was communicating with," Daphne said as she picked it up.

"I think I know!" said Big Dave as he walked out of the woods. In one mighty fist he carried Mr. Peabody, who also had a walkie-talkie.

"Put me down, you lummox!" Mr. Peabody cried. "You can't do this to me!"

"Peabody had Hank pretend to be the marsh monster to scare away visitors. He hoped that would force Mr. Samuels to sell his rafting business," Velma said. "And it almost worked!"

23

With the mystery of the marsh monster solved, the gang was ready to return to their rafting trip. Shaggy and Scooby restocked the raft with plenty of food—including nuts and berries, of course.

"Kids, you saved my business!" Mr. Samuels waved as the gang started off down the river. "I can't thank you enough!"

"And you prevented a greedy man from ruining another precious forest!" called Big Dave.

"Like, it was our pleasure . . . and our duty," said Shaggy with a grin. "Right, Scoob?"

"Scooby-Dooby-Doo," cheered Scooby.